Sound Sense

A. E. TANSLEY B.Sc., M.Ed.

BOOK 1

Illustrated by Jo Chesterman

E. J. ARNOLD & SON LIMITED LEEDS

This is an apple.

Look at the picture. Say the word apple. What sound does it start with?

Here are some words with the a sound in them. See if you can read them:

an and am fat man cat Pat

They all have the a sound in them. They belong to the a family.

EXERCISE 1

Find the a family words and write them in your book.

1	am	and	little	cat	fat
2	Pat	gas	has	him	had
3	rat	dog	man	hat	bag
4	egg	hat	can	cap	sad
5	an	van	sad	bad	fun

EXERCISE 2

Draw a picture of a fat man with his hat and bag.

EXERCISE 3

Look at this picture and in your book
write down the names of the things you
see in the a family. (One of them is man.)

Here is a bottle of ink.

Look at the picture. Say the word ink. What sound does it start with?

Here are more words with the i sound in them. See if you can read them:

in   it   is   if   hill   mill   him   big

They all have the i sound in them. They belong to the i family.

EXERCISE 4

Find the i family words. Write them in your book.

1 big   in   it   is   on
2 fit   him   kiss   here   his
3 bed   miss   fill   if   tin
4 pig   bit   kill   Dick   John
5 did   big   tree   if   mill

EXERCISE 5

Draw a picture of a big red house on a hill.

4

EXERCISE 6

Look at this picture and in your book write down the names of the things you see in the <u>i</u> family.

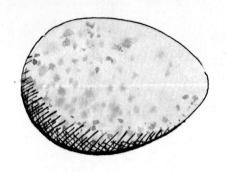

Here is an egg.

Look at the picture. Say the word egg. What sound does it start with?

Here are some more words with the e sound in them. See if you can read them:

hen bell met bed let men well get

They all have the e sound in them.
They all belong to the e family.

EXERCISE 7

Find the e family words. Write them in your book.

1 bed   egg   school leg   wet
2 hen   well   get   big   bell
3 hill   bed   ten   let   wet
4 well   fell   box   pet   fed
5 ten   leg   red   pen   fat

EXERCISE 8

Draw a hen with ten eggs.

EXERCISE 9

Look at the picture and in your book write down the names of the things you see in the _e_ family.

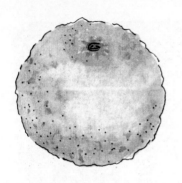

This is an orange.

Look at the picture. Say the word orange. What sound does it start with?

Here are more words with the o sound in them. See if you can read them:

on of off box doll Tom mop not

They all have the o sound in them. They belong to the o family.

EXERCISE 10

Find the o family words. Write them in your book.

1 dog top red lot Tom
2 not Mary doll John got
3 tractor Bob pot off on
4 box God hot off well
5 top pot not sad lot

EXERCISE 11

Draw a picture of John with his dog.

EXERCISE 12

Look at this picture and in your book write down the names of the things you see in the <u>o</u> family.

Here is an umbrella.

Look at the picture.
Say the word
umbrella. What sound
does it start with?

Here are some more
words with the u
sound in them.
See if you can read
them:

us up .fun cup cut but nut tub

They all have the u sound in them.
They belong to the u family.

EXERCISE 13

Find the u family words. Write them in
your book.

1   but   nut   us   ten   gun
2   not   tub   hug   cup   fun
3   cut   this   hum   up   run
4   nut   cup   house   gun   but
5   are   up   nut   hug   tub

EXERCISE 14

Draw a picture of children playing with
a truck.

EXERCISE 15

Look at this picture and in your book
write down the names of the things you
see in the u̲ family.

EXERCISE 16

Find the word in the box which belongs to the same family. Then write the family in your book. The first one is done for you.

1 man am cap has | bit his bag

Answer: man am cap has bag

2 had sad Pat bad | in at if

3 big Dick is it | house here did

4 mill hill fill tin | him pen top

5 hen met bed egg | tree wet full

6 fed red get bell | fun sad let

7 doll on not lot | one dog fat

8 top pot got off | is are box

9 us hug nut up | fit fun red

10 run tub cut cup | Peter men but

EXERCISE 17

Put these words in families.

1 am   big   bill   sad   bit   man   him
   has   in   cap

2 bed   box   lot   bell   egg   God   not
   leg   men   of

3 but   had   bag   nut   cap   and   cut
   tub

4 at   get   dog   had   off   let   an   red
   pot

5 fit   but   is   got   cup   bag   bad   men
   not   met

Now find three more words for these
families.

6 gas   rat   sad   ___ ___ ___
7 tin   if   did   ___ ___ ___
8 hot   Tom   doll   ___ ___ ___
9 fed   ten   sell   ___ ___ ___
10 fun   run   bun   ___ ___ ___

EXERCISE 18

Find the stranger in these families.

1 cap   am   has   fat   bed   had
2 fill bill dog   is   miss big
3 box   of   kiss hot   on   dog
4 and   but   nut   cut   cup   hug
5 egg   bell get   wet   sad   met
6 fat   fill fit   fed   fun   fell here
7 bad   big   bit   box   but   this bell
8 man   mill and   men   miss met

EXERCISE 19

Put in the missing letters.

1 Not good   b-d.
2 Not thin   f-t.
3 This rings   b-ll.
4 To sleep in   b-d.
5 Not out   -n.
6 A pet   d-g
7 Not cold   h-t.
8 A c-p of tea.
9 Part of the body   l-g.
10 We say one m-n but two m-n.

EXERCISE 20

Look at these words:

cap   man   an   ran   can   plan   no   nap
on   lap   pan

Write in your book the ones you can make from <u>aeroplane</u>.

Look at these words:

get   bat   got   let   table   at   sat   bag
cat   bad   met

Write in your book the ones you can make from <u>vegetables</u>.

EXERCISE 21

Put the words in these sentences in the right order.

1 I man. like that
2 lives The dog in a box.
3 bed. of Get out
4 went Mary to school.
5 saw man. I a fat
6 The was egg cup. in a
7 hill. the mill The on is
8 bed. in a sleep I
9 ran hill. The up men the
10 with tea. Fill cup my

Sound Sense   Phonic Check List

This list is for the teacher to use.
Please remove.

Name ....

Date of Birth...........................   Date of   1.....................

                                    checks   2.....................

                                                   3.....................

                                                   4.....................

                                                   5.....................

Vision
Normal/Slightly defective/Defective
Glasses prescribed ..   ..   Yes/No
Glasses worn   ..   ..   Yes/No

Hearing
Normal/Slightly defective/Defective
Hearing loss suspected   ..   Yes/No

Letter Sounds *(taught in Listening to Sounds Books 1 and 2)*

t	n	s	p	g	d	m
l	f	b	r	c	h	w

Blending

a—m   i—f   o—g   u—p   e—t   l—and   s—ing

Sound Sense 1

man	rag	sat	cap	van	bad
will	sit	big	did	it	if
dog	not	mop	got	loss	rocks
men	set	less	pen	beg	well
gun	duck	but	rug	runs	fun
men	sat	sun	fit	moss	bed

Sound Sense 2

see	feet	seed	been	keep
moon	roof	cool	food	noon

Sound Sense 3

take	save	game	late	ape	case
like	mile	nine	ride	time	five
hope	rose	pole	bone	cone	home

Sound Sense 4

car	farm	dark	part	arm
her	over	farmer	sister	letter
fort	corn	nor	lord	worn
call	taller	falling	hall	wall

Sound Sense 5

ship   shed   shame   fish   cash   push
star   stone   stop   stool   cast   lost
thing   three   bath   then   this   those
chop   chest   much   rich   chime   catch

Sound Sense 6

when   which   black   blush   trick   trade
drive   dragon   frame   frost   grass   greed
club   clever   flock   flames   shy   why
baby   penny   eat   seat   dream   steal
dead   weather   instead   ready

Sound Sense 7

rain   tail   nail   day   tray   clay
soil   point   coin   toys   annoy   employ
mouse   pound   count   how   growl   clown
grow   snow   bowl   boat   coal   road
draw   crawl   shawl   author   Paul   cause

Sound Sense 8

light frighten her term furnish nurse
fir birch new fewer stew large page edge
porridge air flair care declare piece
thief believe died flies tried nation
invitation direction selection invasion
confusion graph pheasant telephone
city circle mice wreck know gnaw

Remarks and Recommendations

Date		Teacher's Signature

EXERCISE 22

More than one.

1 We say one hat but several hats.
2 We say one dog but two ____.
3 We say one brother but two ____.
4 We say one egg but six ____.
5 We say one bell but four ____.
6 We say one ____ but many trains.
7 We say one bed but several ____.
8 We say one ____ but two legs.
9 We say one hill but many ____.
10 We say one ____ but three cups.

EXERCISE 23

Write each set of words in your book. Now join with a line words in the same family. The first one is done for you.

1   cap   egg   2   fill   cot
     leg   cut   but   cup
     gun   hat   of   in

3   at   did   4   God   an
     bit   man   and   kiss
     bed   men   bill   off

5   bell has   6   hot   on
     in   let   him   fat
     can   is   cap   his

18

EXERCISE 24

Write each set of words in your book. Now join with a line words beginning with the same letter. The first one is done for you.

1 boy   did
   dog   man
   miss   but

2 egg   cup
   big   end
   can   box

3 let   fill
   hot   house
   fat   little

4 leg   this
   then   on
   off   like

5 cap   lot
   not   cut
   love   night

6 kill   kiss
   bed   dog
   did   big

7 his   mother
   sit   send
   mill   him

8 am   him
   girl   afternoon
   his   got

9 father have
   mad   fit
   hand   moss

10 caravan   wig
    windmill bed
    bell   cab

Now read all the words on this page as quickly as you can.
Read across the page.

EXERCISE 25

Find the stranger in these families.

1 cut   cup   can   dog   cap   cat
2 am   at   boy   and   as   afternoon   apple
3 bad   can   bit   bill   box   bed   but
4 did   had   his   here   hill   has   hot
5 man   mill   met   miss   men   mother   kiss
6 fat   fit   had   fill   fire   football   father
7 lot   like   little   leg   kill   let   lip
8 this   that   like   they   then   than   the
9 dog   dad   doll   tub   did   day   do
10 get   girl   sister   got   go   going   gun

EXERCISE 26

Draw boxes in your book such as the ones below. Put these words in the right boxes.

him book catch man here fit kill kind

had fill bag cut cap big mill kiss

cup but king full miss fat hot morning

h   b   c   f   k   m

him	book	catch	fit	kind	miss

EXERCISE 27

Look at the picture above and write in your book the names of the things you can see there. Then below each word you have written, write other words you have learnt in the same family.

EXERCISE 28

Put these words in families.

1 gas did is has big tin can bad
2 let hot Bob fed get dog pen not
3 God an not kill hill hat bit
   bat on
4 hug us pet men cut sell hum wet
5 bell get lot bill bag off his cap
6 hot leg on did can egg fun
   big cut has
7 am but in bad let fill got of
   cup men

EXERCISE 29

Choose the right word and write the sentence in your book.

1 The (bad, bag) was full of sweets.
2 There is a (dog, did) in the street.
3 I (full, get) out of (but, bed) in the morning.
4 My (cap, can) was blown (of, off) by the wind.
5 Tom fell and (hot, cut) his (leg, got).
6 Jane (met, men) her mother (at, an) ten o'clock.
7 A footballer (his, has) to keep (fit, bit).
8 (Can, Had) you see the (bill, mill) by the river?
9 Did you see the (big, bag) aeroplane come out (of, off) the clouds?
10 Peter (fed, fit) his (dog, doll) every night.

Here is a story for you to read.

Peter lived in an old house by a farm. One day he had to get some eggs for his mother. He went to the farm. When he reached the farm he rang the bell. The farmer came to the door. "Good morning," said Peter. "I have come for some eggs."

"Come in," said the farmer. Peter went in. The farmer's dog Rick was sitting in a box. It had a bad leg. "What is the matter with Rick?" said Peter. "The dog from the mill bit him," said the farmer. "He is nearly better now." "If I saw that dog I would run off," said Peter. The farmer laughed. He gave Peter the eggs and some apples. Peter gave the farmer the right money and went home.

EXERCISE 30

Now you have read the story answer these questions.

1 What is the name of the boy in the story?
2 Where did he live?
3 Why did he go to the farm?
4 What was the name of the farmer's dog?
5 What was the matter with it?
6 What did Peter take home to his mother?
7 How did Rick get a bad leg?
8 What did Peter say he would do if he saw the dog from the mill?

Draw a picture of two dogs playing.

EXERCISE 31

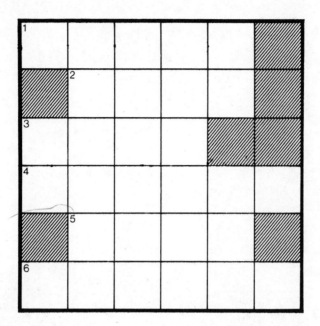

Make a copy of this word puzzle in your book. See if you can put the right words in the right places. All the words you will need are in the story you have just read.

1 The name of the boy in the story is _____.
2 Peter went to the _____.
3 He rang the _____.
4 The _____ came to the door.
5 Peter wanted some _____.
6 The farmer gave Peter the eggs and some _____.

EXERCISE 32

Look carefully at the picture on the opposite page. Write in your book the words for the things you see there beginning with <u>b</u> and beginning with <u>s</u>.

EXERCISE 33

Find the stranger in these families. Write a sentence for each stranger.

1	am	and	fat	tin	gas	sad	Pat	had
2	big	bill	leg	did	fill	kiss	Dick	his
3	box	got	lot	off	on	cap	doll	not
4	but	cup	hug	fun	tub	us	nut	box
5	bed	well	hen	met	red	sell	doll	pet

Read this story about the seaside.

Tom and his sister Pat are at the seaside
for their holiday. They like to be at the
seaside. They play on the sands and swim
in the sea. Tom likes to play with the boys.
They have a bat and ball and play cricket.
Pat plays with her girl friends. They like to
play in the sand-hills but they have a ball
as well.

Today the children were playing with a big red and black ball. The ball went into the sea and they could not get it back. Tom and another boy had to get a sailing-boat to go after it. The ball went out to sea very quickly and the sailing-boat could not catch up with it. The sky was black and the waves were big. The sailing-boat had to go back to the sands. The children's ball was lost and they were sad. Tomorrow they will have to get another one.

EXERCISE 34

Write in your book all the words in the story that begin with <u>s</u>, <u>b</u>, or <u>p</u>.

In the story find five words in the <u>a</u> family, five in the <u>i</u> family, and three in the <u>o</u> family.

Printed in England by E. J. ARNOLD & SON LIMITED Leeds